HE THAT SHOULD COME

Other Plays by
DOROTHY L. SAYERS

THE ZEAL OF THY HOUSE
THE DEVIL TO PAY

HE THAT SHOULD COME

A Nativity Play in One Act

by
DOROTHY L. SAYERS

WIPF & STOCK · Eugene, Oregon

Wipf and Stock Publishers
199 W 8th Ave, Suite 3
Eugene, OR 97401

He That Should Come
A Nativity in One Act
By Sayers, Dorothy L.
Copyright©1939 by Sayers, Dorothy L.
ISBN 13: 978-1-61097-022-8
Publication date 8/1/2011
Previously published by Victor Gollancz Ltd, 1939

Dedicated to the Dorothy L. Sayers Society
that has generously sponsored
the production
of this 2011 series edition

For more information about the DLS Society
please turn to the last page of this book

Introduction to the 2011 Series Edition

On the occasion of the republication of some of Dorothy Leigh Sayers' plays, we pay tribute to a most remarkable person: a literary entrepreneur of no mean order, a lay theologian in an age when it was almost unthinkable for a woman to be acknowledged as a theologian, a thinker who pioneered new ways of engaging audiences with central Christian dogmas as rehearsed in the Church's creeds. The final flowering of her work was connected with her rediscovery of Dante's *Divine Comedy*, which stimulated her to produce some of her finest work, including the play she personally thought was her very best. She did not set out to be a writer of 'religious' drama, but her experience of life through a traumatic era of European history, together with her special talents, made such drama part of her legacy to us.

Born in 1893 at the tail-end of the Victorian era, Dorothy was the only child of well-educated parents. She was baptised in Christ Church, Oxford, (Diocesan Cathedral as well as College Chapel) where her father, an ordained clergyman of the Church of England, was Headmaster of the school which educated the boys who sang in the choir. In 1897 her father accepted a Christ Church living in the 'Fens' (drained, hedgeless farmland) about sixteen miles from Cambridge, and together with her mother, a series of governesses and a brief experience of school from age fifteen, she received an excellent education which suited her particular talents. She emerged into adulthood holding to

Introduction to the 2011 Series Edition

a number of strong convictions, one of which was about the importance of vigorous and clear thinking and speaking about Christian dogma, enlivening the real and varied existences of human beings in all their complexity. Entry to Somerville College, Oxford in 1912 placed DLS among a very favoured few in the Britain of her day, though privilege sheltered no one from the miseries of World War 1 as some of her early published poetry reveals. In any event, her 'Hymn in Contemplation of Sudden Death' (1916)[1] transcends its origins in wartime, though was to come into its own especially in the appalling era of aerial bombing of civilians in the new horrors of World War 11. This is of central importance for the cathedral play written for Lichfield, as we shall see.

So far as World War I is concerned, DLS' detective fiction reflects something of the world of the survivors and the bereaved, and we note here that she never isolated herself from the social and political struggles of her day. Some of her sensitivities are displayed in the development of her portrait of her aristocratic sleuth, Peter Wimsey. He struggles with 'shell-shock' and the memory of having had to give orders which sent so many to their deaths, and as a sleuth he is responsible too for other deaths in a country which still enforced capital punishment. A priority for DLS of course was to find ways of earning her own living, whilst also negotiating a series of love-relationships amongst the somewhat problematic selection of available men of her social class and education post-1918. A man who was not 'marriageable' became the father of her son, her only child, and

---

1 In the selection Hone, R.E.(ed) *Poetry of Dorothy L. Sayers,* Dorothy L. Sayers Society, Swavesey, Cambridge, 1996, pp.78-79; and in Loades, A. (ed) *Dorothy L. Sayers. Spiritual Writings,* SPCK, London, 1993, pp.10-11 from her Opus 1.

Introduction to the 2011 Series Edition

she simply had to earn money to support Anthony, brought up as he was by a trusted friend before he came to know Dorothy as his birth-mother rather than as his 'adoptive' mother. In 1926 DLS married in a Registry Office a divorced war-veteran, 'Mac', whose children from his first marriage did not live with him.

Life was far from easy, what with the political and economic legacy of World War I to contend with, and the lack of sheer political will to make changes for the general good. Few could view the possibility of yet another major conflict with other than the gravest misgivings. Yet it became imperative to destroy the 'Third Reich' with the consequences for the shape of post-war Europe emerging in the latter part of DLS' lifetime. She contributed vigorously to the thinking about the future which needed to be undertaken to bring about change both for the majority of the British population and for international relationships, not least those with defeated countries. Her detective fiction was by no means a trivial distraction from these important tasks, for in it she expressed some of her most passionately held convictions. For central to Christian faith is unequivocal commitment to truth and justice, without these being identified as specifically Christian in her novels. Thus when on honeymoon with Harriet (*Busman's Honeymoon* (1937) she and Peter together face the fact they cannot pick and choose, that they must have the truth no matter who suffers, and that nothing else matters. This will result in a death sentence for the murderer, and another agonising night for Peter as he waits for the eight a.m. moment of the execution, and who knows what consequences for others involved, however marginally. Human justice and the pursuit of truth will never be simple, and the aftermath unpredictable, hardly free of ambiguity and even of a measure of injustice. As Peter says, 'If there *is* a God or a judgement – what next? What have we done?'

Introduction to the 2011 Series Edition

God and judgement were precisely to become the focus of her attention when DLS was caught up into the orbit of Canterbury Cathedral and its Festival of Music and Drama. It was the 'drama' to be associated with the Festival which made it exceptional for its day, given the long-standing suspicion of the pre-Reformation traditions of theatre and liturgy almost wiped out by certain kinds of Protestantism. Canterbury happened to have as its Dean G.K.A. Bell, during the period when its Chapter (governing body) came to think it was time to challenge that suspicion. Having in 1927 founded the Friends of Canterbury Cathedral (an initiative to be followed in many other cathedrals) he found himself with an ally in the person of Margaret Babington, who became the Friends' Steward the following year. Chapter and Friends made possible plays specially commissioned to be performed on the cathedral premises, continuing even after Bell has become Bishop of Chichester in 1929. [2] Bell remains important for understanding DLS' perspective on the cost of the Allied victory in World War II since he became a passionate critic of some aspects of the government's conduct of the war as an Episcopal member of the Upper House of Parliament (the 'Lords').

Both before and after Bell's time as Dean, the plays commissioned for Canterbury Cathedral were by a very distinguished lineage of writers, with T.S. Eliot's *Murder in the Cathedral* (1935) having a most profound impact, given that it was written for the Cathedral in which Thomas a` Becket had been done to death. It also reminded audiences of the possibility of continuing conflict between monarch/government and

2. Jasper, R.C.D. *George Bell: Bishop of Chichester,* OUP, London, 1967. See also Pickering, K. *Drama in the Cathedral. The Canterbury Festival Plays 1928-1948* Churchman Publishing, Worthing, 1985.

Introduction to the 2011 Series Edition

bishop. Following his own contribution on Thomas Cranmer, it was Charles Williams no less who suggested DLS as writer of a play for Canterbury, a choice not necessarily as surprising as some seem to have thought. She had some experience of stage performance and stagecraft from both school and university and a brief experience of school teaching. She had published a short 'poetic drama' *The Mocking of Christ* in her collection of *Catholic Tales and Christian Songs* (1918); *Busman's Honeymoon* had first seen the light of day as a play for the stage (1936), co-authored with another Somervillian, writer Muriel St Clare Byrne, distinguished historian and writer and lecturer at the Royal College of Dramatic Art, and one of DLS' valuable friends in the theatrical world. It was a singular challenge in itself to hit on a subject relevant to Canterbury, and this DLS triumphantly did in choosing to write about the rebuilding of the Cathedral Choir after the fire of 1174, chronicled by a monk, Gervase. Thus *The Zeal of Thy House* came into being, first performed between 12-18 June, 1937, in the Cathedral, and on a London stage in March 1938.

In *Zeal,* some of DLS' convictions are made clear, notably in the character of the architect, William of Sens, the embodiment of the principal human sin, pride. The play is also significant for comprehending the significance for DLS of good work of whatever kind, and her grasp of what it means for human persons to acknowledge themselves as creative agents in the image of the divine Trinity. All this most painfully William has to learn. From this point on, some characteristic features of her work in drama began to emerge. Music specially written for her plays was integral to the liveliness of her presentation of Christian dogma, that in turn further heightened in some cases her scenes of debate and argument, testing vitally important judgements

Introduction to the 2011 Series Edition

about the truth of a situation. Further, her new mode of success as a dramatist was in part the result of her personal humility, willing to take the expert advice of producers and actors as to what would and would not work 'on stage', however admirably written. She was always constructively involved in her productions, in every possible way, making 'cuts' as rehearsals proceeded, whilst frequently restoring her text for publication. Text not used in the original production might or might not be fruitfully used in subsequent ones, depending on context, which might be quite different from its first production.

Such was the success of *Zeal* that DLS was invited to write on Christian dogma for major newspapers, and in addition, received a commission from the then immensely prestigious BBC for a Nativity play (*He That Should Come*) to be broadcast on Christmas Day, 1938. It needs to be recalled that broadcasting was relatively new as a medium for large-scale communication to audiences, and the BBC had high expectations of what it should and should not present to its listeners. Of prime importance for DLS was that she conveyed to her listeners that Christ was born 'into the world', into 'real life', and she had to convey this by sound only. So she re-imagined the world into which Christ was born, engaging not merely with the relevant initial chapters of the first and third gospels (Matthew and Luke) but with centuries of enjoyment of and reflection on the narratives and what had been perceived to be their significance. The main setting is the common courtyard of an inn, in which the characters DLS introduces can grumble about absolutely anything, with differing points of view to be expected from a Pharisee, a merchant and a centurion for example. Joseph plays a central role, and from the world beyond the courtyard the shepherds appear, and it is their gifts which are presented to the child newly born. Finally, we may note that as

Introduction to the 2011 Series Edition

the published text of her Nativity play makes clear, DLS had not been intimidated by criticism that 'long speeches' would be unintelligible to her audiences, since she went on writing them, whilst allowing for them to be 'cut'. Much would depend on audiences and performers, and she had high expectations of all of them.

So successful was *He That Should Come* 'on air', indeed, that DLS was able to respond to a major challenge, namely, the writing of twelve radio plays (the first broadcast of which began on 21 December, 1941) entitled *The Man Born to be King*. These plays remain unique in their conception and execution, not least in wartime, and her vigorous introduction to the published version expounded her intentions as a writer in respect of 'the life of the God Incarnate' which gives us further insight into her theology. Christ 'on air' had to be credible, and so had the particular human beings with whom he had dealings, right through to the scenes when the risen Christ meets with his disciples, surely a major challenge for any dramatist. There were objections in advance of the broadcasts to listeners being able to hear the 'voice' of Jesus of Nazareth', but the fuss gave the plays excellent publicity, and they have remained a most moving exploration of the Gospels and their significance. Interestingly, given that she had limited the presence of the 'Kings' in *He That Should Come* to the 'Prologue' and the very last minutes of that play, in *The Man born to be King* she seized the opportunity further to explore their significance in the very first play of the twelve, 'Kings in Judea'.

That apart, there is an important thread of connection to notice which links DLS' exploration of the character of William in *Zeal* to the 1941 *The Man Born to be King*. William's principal sin was that of pride; that is also true of Judas according to her brilliant analysis and portrayal of him in *The Man Born*

Introduction to the 2011 Series Edition

to be King. Between these two productions one further attempt to explore the roots of human sin in pride had presented itself in *The Devil to Pay*, first performed in Canterbury Cathedral 10-17 June, 1939, with a run on a London stage in the next month. (The outbreak of war in the first days of September was to cut short any further production at least for the time being). Writing this play may well have sharpened up DLS' perception of Judas and of Christ's dealings with him. The theme of *The Devil to Pay* is a re-working of the legend of Faustus- hardly easy to handle. In the first place it had no particular connection with Canterbury Cathedral. In the second place it could be very difficult to persuade an audience to take the 'devil' seriously as the personification of evil, for he was likely to be so entertaining as to 'upstage' the other characters, most importantly, that of Faustus with his besetting sin of pride. DLS had the courage to tackle the legend, because she saw in Faustus a figure which we might say was all too familiar in the political culture of her day, though she does not explicitly make the connection. For we can see behind her Faustus not just the 'impulsive reformer' in all his impatience, but the arrogance of the dictator who turns to unbridled violence as well as to fantasy, with incalculable harm as the result. Her attempt to tackle the full scope of Christ's atonement and redemption lay ahead of her, but there was at least one clue as to her confidence in print, for in her 1916 'The Gates of Paradise', DLS had written of the arrival of Judas accompanied by Christ himself at 'Hades gate' (alluding to the ancient tradition of Christ's raid upon those in bondage to Satan)[3]. It is important to bear this in mind to understand the final scene of *Devil*. Here she has Mephistopheles put in charge

3. See Loades, *Dorothy L. Sayers. Spiritual Writings*, pp.12-15 from her Opus 1.

Introduction to the 2011 Series Edition

of the purging of Faustus and the destruction of the evil for which he has been responsible, but with Faustus himself secure in the promise of his Judge that he will never be forsaken, and that he will be met by his Judge/Saviour at the gates of hell. DLS never denies the depths of human wickedness, but hangs on to a trust in 'redemption' on the very eve of war, of a scope and ferocity she and others at this stage could only fear.

In retrospect, it seems extraordinary, given the progress of World War II in its early stages, that anyone should have had the confidence to suppose that there should be serious consideration given to the shape of social and political life after the war, but to that consideration DLS indeed made a contribution. Thus, for example, in her essay in aesthetics and theology, her 1941 *The Mind of the Maker*, a major point is that if human dignity is to be respected, then social, political and economic life must be so ordered as to express human imagination and creativity. This conviction she spelled out in a series of notably pungent essays. Wartime, however, provoked her into writing one play with which she was richly satisfied, and that was to be *The Just Vengeance* of 1946. The maturity of her theological and dramatic vision now flowered in a play entirely original to herself, born of a number of factors. There was the stimulus Charles Williams' gave to her thinking with his 1943 *The Figure of Beatrice* (Williams himself sadly dying at the tail-end of the war). The result was her re-reading and translation of the whole of Dante's *Divine Comedy*, sometimes working away at this in air-raid shelters. And at this juncture DLS was presented with yet another opportunity to write for a Cathedral. In 1943 it was far from clear when the war might end, or on what terms, but the Chapter of Lichfield Cathedral had the vision and courage to advance plans for a service of Thanksgiving for the

Introduction to the 2011 Series Edition

preservation of the Cathedral, and a Pageant to celebrate seven hundred and fifty years since its foundation, which fell in 1945. Given the inevitable austerities of wartime and its aftermath, it is unsurprising that the whole celebration could not take place in the anniversary year. The invitation to DLS to write a play for Lichfield gave her a priceless opportunity to relate Dante's vision to some deeply troubling features of her own era. (In addition to the play, her appropriation of Dante was to speak most powerfully to the reading public in the years after the war, made possible by the inclusion of her work on 'Hell' and 'Purgatory' in the new Penguin Classics series). It was in Canto xxi of 'Purgatory' that she found the phrase which became the title of *The Just Vengeance*, first performed June 15-26, 1946.

The importance of the phrase was to become clear as DLS wrote *The Just Vengeance*. No pacifist, she had come to the conclusion that the war simply had to be endured. That said, she and others had to reckon with a new dimension of war, which was the deliberate targeting of civilian populations from the air. As World War II developed, Bishop Bell for one became a serious critic of the policy which aimed at the systematic destruction of major German cities one by one, in order to bring the war to an end. For DLS there was a personal dimension to the matter of the bombing of civilians, however. She had learned much from Fraülein Fehmer, a music teacher at school, who had returned home to Frankfurt and become an ardent Nazi. DLS' poem 'Target Area' (1940) imagines her former teacher under the airborne onslaught, rightly recognising that in willing the war she willed the means, though their full horror was yet to be discovered.[4]

The issues she had to some extent explored in her detective fiction DLS now confronted in the light of Christian dogma,

4. Hone, *Poetry*, pp. 140-145.

Introduction to the 2011 Series Edition

that is, that the divine court the human judges as well as the accused alike stand before God, that we are none of us free of guilt. Specifically in *The Just Vengeance* she set herself the task of portraying the Christian doctrine of redemption in the light of the conduct of the war. She set the action in a moment of time as an airman is shot down from his bomber, whilst drawing him into the whole company of those who have and continue to inhabit Lichfield. What she wanted above all to convey was what Dante himself had explored in his understanding of 'just vengeance' in the third and final 'Paradise' section of his *Comedy*. This is that 'redemption', if embraced, leads the sanctified to experience the grace, joy and delight of salvation beyond agony and horror. This third section of Dante DLS knew very thoroughly, and drew on it throughout her play, though never completed her own translation and commentary on it before her own death in 1957. Thus *The Just Vengeance* yields irreplaceable insight into how she imagined the significance of 'redemption' for her own time. The popularity of 'Hell' in the immediate post-war period was understandable – the wicked getting their 'come-uppance' as it were; but the challenge of understanding 'redemption' was the greater. She rose to it magnificently, and was justifiably deeply satisfied with the result.

DLS by this time could draw on long-sustained friendships and trust with the professional actors and theatre people who had worked with her pre-war, with all involved surmounting the difficulties of securing and re-working needed materials in very short supply. Music was integral to the effectiveness of the production, and most fortunately she engaged the skills in costume and scene design of Norah Lambourne, with her extensive first-hand experience of theatre productions (in the 1950s crucial to the re-staging of the York Mystery Plays). She

Introduction to the 2011 Series Edition

was also a key player in the production of DLS' final play, for another commemorative occasion. When Mac, DLS' husband died in 1950, Nora Lambourne moved in with DLS, becoming an invaluable collaborator for *The Emperor Constantine* first performed on Monday 2 July, 1951.

If writing a play for somewhere the size of Lichfield Cathedral was a challenge, an even more problematic context was the Colchester cinema in Festival of Britain year (1951) for Colchester's own festival contribution. The connection of Colchester with Constantine was through a legend which claimed that his mother, Helena, was the daughter of its King, Coel, DLS accepted no restrictions on the size of the cast, nor the time needed to perform the whole play (well over three hours), which displays the complexities of Constantine's achievement and exercise of imperial power, including the debate about Christ's relationship to God at the Council of Nicaea in 325 AD, under Constantine's personal aegis. DLS did not spare her audience the inevitable conflicts of the imperial court, leading to the tragedy of Constantine's destruction of his son. Act 3 is the key, performed in London as *Christ's Emperor*. Like William of Sens, Judas, Faust and the bomber pilot, Constantine has most painfully to realise that the cleansing and redemption of his life comes about through Christ, and that is the precisely the consequence of the dogma he had been instrumental in establishing at Nicaea. It is his mother, Helena, who mediates this truth to him. The play may well be said to be of wider significance exhibiting the problems of connecting the dogmas of a church upheld by state authority, with political life and its associated miseries and triumphs. In its London context of St Thomas' Church off Regent Street the shorter version (*Christ's* Emperor) was set for a challenging run, but the death of George VI in its very first

Introduction to the 2011 Series Edition

week put paid to it. Age-old issues about the human pursuit of truth and justice all too evidently remain.

DLS' work in many genres continued until her unexpected death in 1957. It is thanks to the initiative of Wipf & Stock that we have the texts of these six productions re-published in single volume format, sponsored by the Dorothy L. Sayers Society. Everyone owes an inestimable debt to Dr Barbara Reynolds, engaged life-long with the work of Dante, with DLS' appropriation of Dante, completing the 'Paradise' section of the *Comedy* after DLS' death, editing her letters, writing her biography, and in so many ways stimulating interest in the whole range of work of a most remarkable human being.

The 'religious' plays of DLS, devised for cathedrals, stages and broadcasts were written to be adaptable for performance in many different contexts. They are meant to be exciting, stirring, challenging, memorable, getting everyone involved at the most serious level with issues of inescapable and permanent importance.

Ann Loades
Tayport, Scotland
April 2011

Synopses of the Religious Drama by Dorothy Sayers

THE ZEAL OF THY HOUSE

Dorothy L. Sayers took her inspiration from a monk's account of the fire of 1174, and the subsequent rebuilding of Canterbury Cathedral Quire. She portrays William of Sens, the chosen architect, as eaten away by pride in his splendid work, unable to give glory to God for his achievement. Enacted in the presence of a group of graciously influential Archangels, the play reveals the carelessness of some of the monks, resulting in the terrifying fall that cripples William. His agony brings him to repentance and gratitude before God, and finally to the renunciation of his role, leaving the completion of the re-building to others.

First performed on June 12, 1937; first published by V.Gollancz in June 1937.

HE THAT SHOULD COME

In this first of her plays for religious broadcasting, Dorothy L. Sayers wanted to convince listeners of the truth that Christ was born into our deeply problematic world, in his case, in territory overrun by an army of occupation. Although framed as it were

Synopses of the Religious Drama by Dorothy Sayers

by the voices of the three 'wise men' asking whether the birth of a particular child could possibly fulfil their desires, the focus of the play is on the conflict of opinion (about roads, taxes, and so forth) expressed by those in the courtyard of the inn at Bethlehem. Joseph is given a most significant role, and it is the shepherds whose gifts are presented when the Holy Family is revealed.

First broadcast on December 25, 1938; first published by V.Gollancz in November 1939.

THE DEVIL TO PAY

Dorothy L. Sayers re-worked the legend of Faust as a serious 'comedy', presenting Faust as one who chooses wicked means as an end to an admirable goal: the relief of suffering (while becoming entirely focussed on his own supposed satisfactions). In the last scene, in the Court of Heaven, Azrael, angel of the souls of the dead, claims Faustus' soul, opposing Mephistopheles' claim. With the knowledge of good and evil returned to him, Faustus finally accepts that his evil must be cleansed, with Mephistopheles serving as the agent of that purgation. Faustus accepts his need for cleansing, trusting that the divine Judge/Court President, will indeed in mercy meet him at the very gates of hell, finally redeemed.

First performed on June 10, 1939; first published by V.Gollancz in June 1939.

THE MAN BORN TO BE KING

In twelve plays for broadcasting at monthly intervals, Dorothy L. Sayers drew on material from all four Gospels,

Synopses of the Religious Drama by Dorothy Sayers

keeping the theme of Jesus of Nazareth's divine kingship in focus throughout, while locating him firmly in the social and political context of his time. The first half cover episodes that precede the final journey to Jerusalem and the latter half primarily deal with Passion Week themes. It is on the simplicity and profundity of Jesus' words in the Fourth Gospel especially that Sayers drew on in her own writing for the 'voice' of Jesus 'on air'. The plays gave her an opportunity to explore the many gospel characters surrounding Jesus, not least that of Judas. And beyond the utter sorrow of Jesus' death, the King comes into his own in the garden of resurrection.

The first play was broadcast on December 21, 1941, with the rest at four-weekly intervals thereafter, concluding on October 18, 1942; first published by V.Gollancz in 1943.

THE JUST VENGEANCE

In this play Dorothy L. Sayers addressed the crimes and problems of human life, especially those of the victors in war, in an entirely novel way, by precipitating an airman in the very moment of his death back into the company of citizens of the 'City', in this case, Lichfield. The citizens range from Adam and Eve (Adam himself the inventor of the axe which kills Abel) together with other biblical characters in the history of redemption brought to new life as members of the City, (e.g. Judas is a common informer). Others bear burdens of shame, toil, fear, poverty and ingratitude. Former inhabitants (e.g. George Fox, Dr. Johnson) help the airman to see that no more than they can he shift the burden of his guilt and grief that they all share.

There is but one remedy, to join the 'Persona Dei' carrying his cross, finding indeed that he bears their burdens for them. The 'Persona Dei' is finally seen in resurrection and glory.

First performed on June 15, 1946; first published by V.Gollancz in June 1946. Broadcast: March 30, 1947.

THE EMPEROR CONSTANTINE

A brief 'Prologue' by the 'Church' introduces the career of Constantine (from A.D. 305-337) with scenes from the empires of both west and east, concentrating on Constantine's progress to imperial power and inevitably in religious belief. He discovers Christ to be the God who has made him his earthly vice-regent as single Emperor. Summoning the Council of Nicaea at 325, an invigorating debate results in the acceptance of Constantine's formula that Christ is 'of one substance with God'. The implications of the creed of Nicaea are revealed in the last part of the play in which it is his mother, Helena, who brings him to the realisation that he needs redemption by Christ for his political and military life as well as for the domestic tragedy which has resulted in the death of his son.

First performed on July 2, 1951; first published by V. Gollancz in August 1951. A shortened version entitled *Christ's Emperor* was performed at St Thomas' Church, Regent Street in February 1952.

NOTE TO PRODUCERS

"HE THAT SHOULD COME" was originally written for broadcasting, and its adaptation for the stage has presented certain difficulties, owing to the difference between the two media. The main dialogue seemed to require little alteration; the trouble begins with the background and subsidiary characters.

The intention of the play is to show the birth of Christ against its crowded social and historical background, and for that purpose it was necessary to make real to the audience the bustling and variegated life of an autonomous province in the great, sprawling, heterogeneous Roman Empire of the first century. The inn was to be shown crowded with as many and various types as possible—the orthodox Pharisee, with his rigidly national religious views; the Hellenised Jew, with his liberal outlook influenced by contact with Rome; the Greek, with his intellectual pliability and sceptical detachment; the trader, treading warily on thorny political ground and anxious to give offence to nobody; the peasant, earning a precarious livelihood amid the hurly-burly of conflicting forces perpetually threatening his small security; behind them all, the ruthless tyranny of a self-made Oriental despot, ruling a strange mixed province of strict Jews in the south and fierce heathen tribes in the north; and behind him again, the iron strength of Rome, legal, military, and imperial, caring nothing for internal politics or

NOTE TO PRODUCERS

religious disputes so long as her tributaries kept the peace and paid the taxes.

To obtain this effect, the scene was laid, not with particular reference to the traditional cave at Bethlehem, but in an Oriental inn of the usual kind, consisting of a two-storied rectangular building surrounding an open courtyard, somewhat after the style of a college quadrangle. In the centre of the courtyard was a raised platform, on which the travellers sat or lay, surrounded by their luggage. The ground floor of the building consisted of a series of vaulted stables carrying the chambers on the first floor, over which was a flat roof. The inn had a gate, which was barred at night against marauders. The inn is supposed to be situated on the road going up from Bethlehem to Jerusalem.

It thus became possible to introduce all the necessary characters quite plausibly into this common courtyard. For the purpose of a broadcast, the crowded condition of the inn was sufficiently indicated by introducing a few allusions to the throng of travellers and by fading in a babble of voices at appropriate points in the dialogue. Attention was easily focused on one point or another of the scene by conveying the suggestion of the character picking his way among the assembled travellers, and by inserting a line to announce his arrival at the gate, the stable, the Centurion's post, and so forth.

This scene, so excellently suitable for a broadcast, at once offers difficulties in the theatre, where the crowd of travellers has not merely to be indicated, but to be seen in action and kept continually on the stage. Having once introduced the characters, you

NOTE TO PRODUCERS

cannot move them off and leave the stage clear, because it is the whole point of the story that the inn was crowded to suffocation and that there *was* no clear space. In consequence, the stage being thus crowded and obliged to remain crowded, it becomes very difficult to move the actors naturally from one point to another, or to give the " background characters " anything sensible to do without distracting attention from the speakers. A subsidiary difficulty was to bring the various groups, as they became important to the action, into a sufficiently commanding position and not leave them isolated up-stage or blocked in inconvenient doorways to right and left.

I have coped with these difficulties as well as I could, bearing in mind that the play may be acted by repertory or amateur companies having at their disposal stages of widely varying dimensions and lighting equipment. The play as here arranged allows for the largest stage and the largest company that are likely to be available. There are fifteen characters necessary for the performance of the dialogue; to these I have added nine subsidiary characters to bring the cast up to twenty-four. These, with a proper allowance of baggage and other properties, should be enough to produce a quite convincing crowd on a stage of reasonable dimensions. The actual " crowding-space " of the stage will be governed by the size of the central rostrum, where this is available, and the scenery or curtains can be brought in accordingly.

Where the stage is insufficiently large to accommodate the full cast, the minor characters can be cut down at will, and the " background " dialogue altered to fit the situation. The guiding principle to be taken

NOTE TO PRODUCERS

is to ask: How many people will give an effect of real crowding on this particular stage? and to work from that figure. Where the smallness of the stage or of the available company requires the cast to be limited to the fifteen principal characters, the Landlady's call for a midwife can be answered from off-stage, as though from the upper storey of the inn.

In the absence of built scenery, the play can very suitably be performed in curtains; an inner set of these can be bunched so as to suggest the archways alluded to in the text. The stage directions allow for either one or two archways on either side, according to the depth of the stage. Where there are two, the directions "right" and "left" should be taken to refer to the lower entrances and the directions in brackets (R.U.) and (L.U.) to the upper entrances.

If the play is performed in a church without scenery or curtains, it is suggested that the entrance to the choir should be screened off and opened to display the tableau of the Holy Family. The exits right and left can then be suitably made into the aisle or transept as the case may be, whose arches will supply the appropriate suggestion.

What is done with the Kings during the main action of the play depends upon the means at the producer's disposal. I have made one or two suggestions, according as the building is furnished with one or more sets of front curtains and with more or less elaborate front-of-house lighting. If the play is given in a church without curtain, the Kings might very suitably enter from the West door, through the darkened nave, and be lit by a single spot or a strong electric torch till the time comes to light the whole scene. It would

NOTE TO PRODUCERS

then be symbolically appropriate that they should make their exit eastward, if possible, up either side of the choir towards the Sanctuary, with the light of a torch going before them to represent the Star.

The action of the play should take about an hour. If it is found too long, the Greek Gentleman's Song and the second verse of the Soldiers' Marching Song may be cut. In the original broadcast the long speeches of the Kings were also omitted; but this cut is not recommended. As accompaniment to the songs, a harp, lute, guitar (if that is the best available), or other *plucked* string instrument will give the right effect; orchestral or organ accompaniments are quite unsuitable. A piano would do at a pinch; a harpsichord still better.

The whole effect and character of the play depend on its being played in an absolutely natural and realistic style. Any touch of the ecclesiastical intonation or of " religious unction " will destroy its intention. The whole idea in writing it was to show the miracle that was to change the whole course of human life enacted in a world casual, inattentive, contemptuous, absorbed in its own affairs and completely unaware of what was happening: to illustrate, in fact, the tremendous irony of history. It may be found advisable to make this point clear to the actors before they start, lest some preconceptions as to what is or is not " reverent " in a Nativity Play should hamper the freedom of their performance. I feel sure that it is in the interests of a true reverence towards the Incarnate Godhead to show that His Manhood was a real manhood, subject to the common realities of daily life; that the men and women surrounding Him were living human beings, not just characters in a story; that, in short, He was born, not into " the Bible ", but into the world. That an audience will take the play in this spirit is proved to me by the various letters I received after the first broadcast. As one man in a country village put it, " It's nice to think that people in the Bible were folks like us." And another correspondent: " None of us realised before how much we had just *accepted* the story without properly visualising it. It . . . brought home to us as never before the *real* humanity of Jesus." There will always be a few voices raised to protest against the introduction of " reality " into religion; but I feel that the great obstacle in the path of Christianity to-day is that to so many it has become unreal, shadowy, " a tale that is told ", so that it is of the utmost importance to remind people by every means in our power that the thing actually happened—that it is, and was from the beginning, closely in contact with real life.

I found that the broadcasting company really enjoyed playing in this little piece of " real-life " drama, and hope that it will prove itself " good theatre " in a different medium. Since I have had no chance to try out the adaptation with actors upon a stage, I shall be very glad if producers will let me or my agents know how it works out in practice, and what devices their ingenuity has used to get over the obvious " snags " in presentation, so that, if necessary, I may revise the text in the light of their experience.

DOROTHY L. SAYERS.

"*He That Should Come*" was first performed in the original broadcast version on the London National Transmission from Broadcasting House on Christmas Day, 1938, with the following cast:

CASPAR	Harcourt Williams
MELCHIOR	William Devlin
BALTHAZAR	Robert Adams
MERCHANT	Henry Longhurst
GREEK GENTLEMAN	Robert Farquharson
CENTURION	Gordon McLeod
LANDLORD	Philip Wade
LANDLADY	Marjorie Fielding
JOSEPH	Patrick Curwen
MARY	Gwen Catley
JEWISH GENTLEMAN	Raf de la Torre
1ST SHEPHERD	Wallace Evenett
2ND SHEPHERD	Frederick Peisley
3RD SHEPHERD	Pat Laffan

Barry Faber, Angela Kirk
and the B.B.C. Singers

The Music composed by ROBERT CHIGNELL

Producer: VAL GIELGUD

The present version has been adapted for Stage Performance by the author. The music may be had on loan from Dorothy Allen, 32 Shaftesbury Avenue, W.1 (acting in association with Messrs. Pearn, Pollinger & Higham, Ltd.), to whom all applications for performing rights should be addressed.

DRAMATIS PERSONAE

Persons of the Prologue and Epilogue

CASPAR, King of Chaldea, an aged man.
MELCHIOR, King of Pamphylia, a man in the prime of life.
BALTHAZAR, King of Ethiopia, a young negro.

Persons of the Play

THE JEWISH MERCHANT, a stout man with a plummy voice.
THE PHARISEE, a tall, thin and severe man.
THE YOUNG GREEK GENTLEMAN, a suave young man, with a foreign accent.
THE JEWISH GENTLEMAN, the " Oxford graduate " of the period.
THE ROMAN CENTURION, the very best type of non-commissioned officer.
THE LANDLORD, a square-built, husky-voiced person, with a wholesome terror of the law.
THE LANDLADY, a harassed woman with a shrill voice.
JOSEPH, a mild, courteous man, with the plain dignity of the skilled artisan.
MARY, a serene, sweet-voiced woman, with an air of great stillness about her.
1ST SHEPHERD, an elderly peasant.
2ND SHEPHERD, a middle-aged peasant.
3RD SHEPHERD, a young peasant.

MINOR PERSONAGES

Two Roman Soldiers—A Husband and Wife—A Father, Mother and Little Boy—A Manservant—A Maidservant.

PROLOGUE

[*The Prologue is played upon the fore-stage. If there is a front curtain as well as tableaux curtains, it rises to discover* MELCHIOR. *If not,* MELCHIOR *should enter in darkness before the curtain, and a steel spot be gradually turned up to reveal him, sitting left of stage.*

    MELCHIOR (*sings to the tinkling of a lute*)

High upon the holy tree
    (*Whither away, love?*)
Dragon-guarded ceaselessly
    (*Whither away?*)
There hangs the splendour sought of old,
The lamb, the ram, the fleece of gold
    (*Colchis, O Colchis,*
    Give me my heart again!)

Enter CASPAR. *He speaks out of the darkness, right.*

CASPAR

What traveller is that,
Sitting and singing beside the desert fountain,
Challenging with his frail music
This blinding silence of silver midnight,
Brighter than moonlight, whiter than sunlight,
This unaccustomed miracle of sevenfold starlight?

HE THAT SHOULD COME

MELCHIOR (*rising*)

I am a Greek,
Born in the West, on the shores of the Mediterranean,
A European, in fact. I am not afraid of a thing
Merely because it is unaccustomed. Our instinct
Is to challenge destiny. That is why I am here.
There is a muttering among the oracles,
A song in the poets' mouths. They tell of a child
That shall shake off the iron yoke of necessity,
Bring back the golden age and the brave Saturnian
    reign.
He hath set up his sceptre in the sky; very well;
It is my duty to find out the truth about this;
I am a ruler, I owe my people the truth;
And on my people's behalf I have ridden hither,
Melchior, King of Pamphylia, surnamed " the Just ",
Following the Star.

CASPAR (*coming forward into the light*)

I am an astrologer; I have watched from the high
    towers
Nightly the signs of heaven stride
Through the houses of fate in the turning horoscope.
I have seen this new star turn and burn
Slowly out of the east, leaping from cusp to cusp,
Till now it sits ruling the house of life;
And I have asked myself what god should be born
From this astonishing conjunction. Therefore am I
    come,
Caspar, King of Chaldea, surnamed " the Wise ",
Following the Star.

Melchior

Listen! the sound of bells—
Another traveller comes, riding upon a camel,
With a train of swift camels. His face is as the night,
His eyeballs glint white in the night of his face. Who's
    there?

[*Enter* BALTHAZAR, *right, and speaks out of the darkness.*

Balthazar

Out of the darkness, out of the desert,
Beyond the secret springs of the Nile
I have seen the fire of desire flare in the zenith
Scaring the crocodiles under the shadow of the pyra-
    mids.
The dusky gods have trembled, the witch-dancers are
    struck down
In the midst of their dances.
A cry is gone up in the halls of the dead, from the seven
    gates of the dead,
The cry of Isis over Osiris slain,
The birth-cry of Horus.
This is the end or else the beginning of all things,
And sorrow either way, between a cry and a cry;
  [*He comes into the light.*
Therefore I come, seeking the soul of sorrow,
Balthazar, King of Ethiopia, surnamed " the Servant ",
Following the Star.

Melchior

Yonder it stands, and yonder, by my reckoning,
The City of Jerusalem, a twelve-days' journey hence.

CASPAR

Strangely are we met, Wisdom, Justice, and Service,
Following the Star, seeking we know not what.

BALTHAZAR (*standing between them*)

Magi, my brothers, let us take counsel of the crystal—
I hold it in my dark hand, shining against the darkness
of my hand;
Let the crystal display to us what shall be the end of the
journey.

[*He kneels down.*

CASPAR

Will he come, will he speak at last, the ultimate
wisdom,
The unalterable truth behind and above the appearance?
I have studied all the philosophies, and now I am old;
Every day I care less about life and death, sorrow and
happiness—
I ask only that what we see shall correspond to something,
Beautiful or terrible, but constant in some way or other.
We build the house of thought, stone upon stone,
And just as we have finished the topmost pinnacle
There comes a grinning doubt and pulls away the
foundation.
One has to assume something before one can think at
all,
If it is only the validity of one's own thinking,
Or one's immediate perceptions,

Or the numerical proposition that two and two make four.
Give me a single integer and I will build up the universe,
Star upon flaming star, and the singing orbits of planets,
And the springing sap, and the life in the blood, and splendour,
Beauty and love and grief and the promise of immortality—
Only, it is from the universe that I deduce the integer
From which to deduce the universe again;
And thus all knowledge is only a vicious circle
Ceaselessly spinning upon the axis of nothing.
Nor can I even be sure that everything,
Including myself, is nothing,
Since it is in myself that I find the all and the nothing;
And it may be that nothingness is in itself an illusion,
The last illusion of all.

[CASPAR *kneels.*

MELCHIOR

I will accept the illusions;
I do not mind whether they are illusions or not,
I am not interested in dogma, I want a religion that works;
What I look for is good government,
A reasonable way of life, within the terms of the illusion.
If there is nothing at the end of it, be it so—there is nothing;
But in the meantime, can we not achieve a little decency,
A little dignity,
A pattern of some kind, such as we make so easily
For a curtain or a cornice, which does not matter at all,

But cannot make for our lives, which matter a great deal,
Or, at any rate, seem to matter? Always we hope for
    a formula,
The master-word, the philosopher's stone, the elixir of
    life,
The abracadabra that settles everything—
The formula of empire, the formula of liberty,
The formula of isolation, the formula of collective
    security,
The formula of discipline, the formula of self-expression,
And all the rest of it.
Always we are disappointed, always there are com-
    plications,
There does not seem to be any simple rule
To make things go smoothly.
We have wasted too much time in quarrelling and
    asking questions;
Let us put our trust in a personality
Capable of commanding our loyalty—strength
And leadership, and calm hands ordering everything,
And the government shall be upon his shoulder, lord
    of lords, and king of kings.

[MELCHIOR *kneels.*

BALTHAZAR

How much you need to content you!
The wisdom that sets the soul beyond the reach of
    suffering,
The power to abolish suffering. I am more humble;
I do not mind being ignorant and unhappy—
All I ask is the assurance that I am not alone,
Some courage, some comfort against this burden of
    fear and pain.

I am a servant, born of the seed of Ham,
The oppressed, the accurst;
My skin is black with the punishing fury of the sun.
About my palaces the jungle creeps and whines,
Famine and plague are my fireside companions,
And beyond the circle of the fire, the glare of hungry eyes.
The lion sits by the water-hole, where the women go down to wash,
In the branches crouches the leopard.
I look out between the strangling branches of the vine and see
Fear in the east, fear in the west; armies
And banners marching and garments rolled in blood.
Yet this is nothing, if only God will not be indifferent,
If He is beside me, bearing the weight of His own creation;
If I may hear His voice among the voices of the vanquished,
If I may feel His hand touch mine in the darkness,
If I may look upon the hidden face of God
And read in the eyes of God
That He is acquainted with grief.

Caspar

Gather the rays of the Star into the crystal.

Melchior

Look, and see the shape of things afar off.

Balthazar

Listen, and hear the shadows speak in the crystal.

[*A murmur of movements and voices behind the tableaux curtains or gauzes.*]

Caspar

See! the light stirs and blurs to a pale cloud in the crystal—

Melchior

Like an opal, with green fire darting and parting at the core!

Balthazar

Look and listen! the life of the world is born in the heart of the crystal.

[*The spot is gradually dimmed down upon the* Three Kings, *who may then make their exit in the black-out, or, if preferred, they may remain upon the stage throughout the action of the play.*

If gauzes are available, the lights behind them will be brought up slowly on the dimmers as the spot fades during the Kings' *last three lines, and the gauzes taken up in succession during the opening conversation in the inn.*

Where there are no gauzes, the tableaux curtains will be opened at cue on the fully-lit scene.

Suggested Lighting: *Steel in the front spots; blue and white in No. 3 batten; steel arena flood on check centre for star over stable; amber flood shining down staircase left (L.U.) and steel flood through doorway to gate, right; red light in braziers, reinforced by spots if necessary. The impression to be conveyed is of an unroofed courtyard on a brilliant star-light night.*

The Stable of the Nativity can be lit by a white batten, or by a couple of baby spots centred upon the Holy Child.

HE THAT SHOULD COME

[*The voices of the travellers are heard before the curtains are opened. The five following pages must be played at top speed.*

MERCHANT

Landlord! Landlord!

ANOTHER VOICE (*fading off, left*)

Three of us and six servants, and see that the brown mule gets a good rub down.

PHARISEE

Landlord! Landlord!

MANSERVANT

T'ch, t'ck! Git over there!

MERCHANT

Held up twice between here and Jericho. What the Government thinks it's doing. . . .

1ST SOLDIER

Best of three!

2ND SOLDIER

My belt against your Persian dagger.

JEWISH GENTLEMAN

Look sharp, my lad, with that jug of wine.

MANSERVANT

Yes, sir! Yes, sir! Coming in a minute.

WIFE

Really, Ezra, am I to stand here all night?

[*The curtains open. The centre of the stage is occupied by a rectangular platform, its down-stage edge lying just behind the curtain line. A passage runs round the back and both sides at stage level. At the back are three archways, leading to the stables; their entrances (R.B., C.B. and L.B.) are concealed by rough hangings of sacking. Similar archways, at the sides of the stage, lead, on the right to the gateway of the inn, on the left to a staircase going up to the roof. (*NOTE.*—If the depth of the stage permits, there may be two of these entrances either side, in which case the lower right entrance will lead to the gate, and the upper left to the stairs. See page 8.) Behind the centre archway at the back is the Stable of the Nativity, the floor of which is raised somewhat above the level of the platform. Both platform and passage-way are obstructed by baggage of every description—mattresses, saddle-bags, saddles, cooking utensils, and so forth. On the right, the* GREEK GENTLEMAN *has just entered, and is working his way centre. Near right entrance sprawl a couple of* ROMAN SOLDIERS, *entertaining themselves with a dice-box and a large pot of beer. Well down, and a little right of centre, the* PHARISEE *is sitting, with the* LANDLORD *in attendance. Just above centre, a* PEASANT FATHER *and* MOTHER *have established themselves with their* LITTLE BOY; *a* MAID-SERVANT *is filling their pitcher with water and giggling at* FATHER. *Right of centre the respectable* HUSBAND *and* WIFE *are standing surrounded by luggage, and looking rather helpless. Above and left of them stands the* MER-

CHANT, *and a little above between them and the family party stands the* ROMAN CENTURION, *checking over the papers of the* JEWISH GENTLEMAN. *Right back a* MAN-SERVANT *is carrying a bundle of fodder into the stable. All through the opening dialogue the* PHARISEE *sits severely silent, reading a scroll.*

HUSBAND

Of course not, my dear. (*He beckons to the* MAID-SERVANT.) Here, girl, here! (*The* GIRL *is being chucked under the chin by the* FATHER, *and pays no attention.*)

MAIDSERVANT

Give over, now, do!

LANDLADY (*entering left (L.U.), shrilly*)

Now then, you lazy baggage! Water and towels for the party upstairs.

MAIDSERVANT

Yes, madam. (*She hurries off, left (L.U.).*)

HUSBAND (*trying in vain to detain her*)

The service in these inns is disgraceful!

WIFE

Is there nobody here to attend to a lady?

LANDLORD (*coming upstage*)

Wife, here's a lady wants you.

LANDLADY

Gentleman upstairs wants these cleaned. (*She dumps a cloak and a pair of boots into his arms. He takes them off, right (R.U.).*) Yes, madam? (*She attends to* WIFE.)

MANSERVANT (*coming down to* JEWISH GENTLEMAN *with wine*)

Sorry to keep you waiting, sir. We're run off our feet with the rush.

BOY

Mother! Mother! I want a piece of cake.

[CENTURION *goes centre and speaks to* GREEK GENTLEMAN.

MOTHER

Cake, indeed! You'll wait till supper's ready.

GREEK GENTLEMAN

Native of Bethlehem? Heaven forbid! We're going on to Jerusalem. (*He comes down to* MERCHANT.)

FATHER (*catching* MANSERVANT *as he returns centre*)

Give us a hand with the pack-saddle, can't you? (*They go up towards stable, back (L.B.). The* CENTURION *has meanwhile crossed right, and is watching the* SOLDIERS *at their game.*)

1ST SOLDIER

The gods to aid! (*Throws dice.*) Venus, by Bacchus!

HE THAT SHOULD COME

2ND SOLDIER

Curse it! You've cleaned me out. (*Drinks.*)

1ST SOLDIER

That's no reason to swill all the beer. (*Snatches pot from him. Scuffle.*)

WIFE

Find us a nice quiet spot, away from those drunken soldiers.

[*Her* HUSBAND *leads her across left, above* MERCHANT *and his baggage.*

MANSERVANT (*off, back*)

Steady, hoss, steady. So-ho there!

JEWISH GENTLEMAN

Hey, you! Take those damned camels where my horse can't wind 'em! (*He dashes out (R.B.).*)

MERCHANT (*down, left*)

Taxes! that's what it means, more taxes! Why else should they take a census? Just idle curiosity on the part of the Imperial Government?

GREEK GENTLEMAN

Well, sir, I imagine they must find occupation for the staff at the Home Office. Besides, the Emperor takes a great interest in vital statistics.

Merchant

Vital statistics my foot! They mean to clap on a poll-tax, you see if they don't. As if we weren't squeezed and badgered enough already, what with Imperial taxes and the King's taxes, customs, excise, land-tax, house-tax, and now this monstrous new stamp-duty on sales. Trade, sir, trade is the life-blood of the country, and they're strangling it, deliberately doing all they can to strangle it, with these iniquitous exactions. But there! I can tell by your speech you're a foreigner. Perhaps they manage things better where you come from. (*Sits on* Husband's *baggage, left.*)

Greek Gentleman

I am a Greek, sir; Philip is my name. I am travelling to Jerusalem with letters of introduction to the King's historian. I dabble a little in letters—oh! very amateurishly, I assure you—and have foolishly undertaken to write a trifling study of social and economic conditions in the Roman provinces. Anything I can learn about the effect of legislation on commerce is of great assistance to my ignorance.

[Landlord *re-enters right (R.U.) and checks papers with* Centurion, *they move up back.*

Merchant

Well, you can put it in your book, sir, that the effect of this kind of legislation is disastrous. I don't mince words, I say disastrous. Between the King and the Emperor, we're between the upper and the nether millstones. The King pampers the labouring classes at the expense of respectable citizens, and the Emperor makes it his business to thrust a crowbar into the wheels at every opportunity. . . .

Husband

Confound you, sir, that's my bag you're sitting on. (*He jerks his luggage away and returns up left.*)

Merchant

. . . It's a scandal to disturb honest tradesmen at the busiest time of the year, and send them trapesing up and down the country, just to get themselves registered at some infernal village where they had the misfortune to be born. Here's weeks of valuable time wasted—not to mention the peril to life and limb.

[Landlady *works up and off, left (L.U.).*

Greek Gentleman

Certainly the roads are in a shocking state—and terribly congested.

[Jewish Gentleman *comes out of stable (L.B.) and goes in again (R.B.).*

Merchant

Congested? That's nothing. They're not safe, my good sir, they're not safe! Bandits and revolutionaries lurking in every thicket. My heart was in my mouth all the way, and we passed some most ruffianly-looking characters in the hill-country near Beth-Horon. I suppose, by the way, you don't know anybody who's travelling back in that direction, and would permit me to join his company?

Greek Gentleman

I'm afraid not. I'm a stranger here myself, you know. But we might ask the Roman centurion over there. He seems to be checking up on the arrivals.

Merchant

Thank you, thank you, that's an excellent suggestion. Will you add to your kindness by accompanying me?
    don't like the look of some of these people—I'm sure they'd pick your purse as soon as look at you. (*They move up centre. To* Wife.) Excuse me, madam, I wish to speak to the Centurion. (*To* Husband.) Allow me, sir. (*They grudgingly make way for him.*) This place is dreadfully overcrowded. (*He encounters* Manservant *and* Father, *returning from the stable, their shoulders laden with a pack-saddle, goatskins, cooking utensils, etc.*) Pray let me pass, my good fellows. (*They shove past him, thrusting him aside upon the* Boy, *who utters a sharp yell.*) Oh, I beg your pardon, I didn't see your little boy; I hope I've not hurt him.

Mother (*venomously*)

Some people want all the place to themselves!

[*In the meantime, the* Centurion *has moved across with the* Landlord *to the left upper corner of the stage, and is as far off as ever. The* Merchant, *with a despairing cry, darts after him in this new direction, and becomes involved with the* Landlady *and the* Maidservant, *who enter*

HE THAT SHOULD COME

left (L.U.), bringing some cooked food to the HUSBAND *and* WIFE.

MERCHANT

Dear, dear, I'm sorry. How clumsy of me! Pardon, pardon.

LANDLADY (*looking daggers*)

Granted, I'm sure.

[*The* CENTURION *and* LANDLORD *come half-way down by passage, left; thé* MERCHANT *following. The* GREEK GENTLEMAN, *smiling imperturbably, insinuates himself neatly through the crowd in the* MERCHANT'S *wake, and everybody thinks him charming.*

MERCHANT (*arriving at last*)

Good evening, Captain. Can you spare me just a moment of your time?

CENTURION

In one minute, sir. Here, landlord, all these papers seem to be in order. I shouldn't think there'd be any more arrivals now. You'd better close the gates.

LANDLORD

Yes, Captain. Thank you, Captain. I don't see how we could take anybody else if they did come. (*Shouting.*) Porter, bar the gates!

PORTER (*shouting off, right*)

There's another party here wants to come in.

Landlord

What's that?

Porter

There's a party here with a donkey. I've told 'em there ain't no room.

Landlord

All right, I'll come myself. (*He comes down left and starts to cross behind* Pharisee, *turning as he goes to speak to the* Centurion.) There wasn't anything further, was there, Captain?

Centurion

No, that's all right. Carry on.

[*Exit* Landlord, *right.*

Now, Master Merchant, what can I do for you?

Merchant

I was wondering, Captain, whether you knew of any one who would be returning by way of Beth-Horon?

Centurion

Well, let me see, now. Why, yes, there's a young gentleman going through that way to-morrow as far as Lydda. I forget his name, but you'll find him somewhere about, wearing a Roman dress and a green cloak.

MERCHANT

Thank you, Captain, thank you. I am going to Lydda myself.

[*Re-enter, right,* LANDLORD. *He backs in, making expostulatory gestures.* JOSEPH *follows, pleading with him.* MARY *comes quietly behind* JOSEPH.

Is he a wealthy gentleman, with plenty of armed servants? Do you think he would permit me to join his party?

LANDLORD

No, no, no, I tell you.

JOSEPH

Yes, but do listen a moment . . .

[LANDLADY *works across to them.*

CENTURION (*to* MERCHANT)

Couldn't say, I'm sure, sir. You'd better ask him. (*His eye has been caught by the little disturbance on the other side of the stage.*) Excuse me, the landlord seems to be having a spot of bother over there. I'll have to go and keep an eye on it. Now then, good people, out of my way, please! (*He strides unceremoniously across the centre of the stage.*)

MANSERVANT (*obsequiously*)

Clear the way for the Captain!

MOTHER (*snatching her* BOY *out of the way*)

Look out, here's the Centurion coming.

HE THAT SHOULD COME

FATHER (*finding himself accidentally blocking the* CENTURION'S *path and being unceremoniously shoved aside*) Beg your pardon, Captain. (*Aside.*) Damn your Roman insolence!

CENTURION (*whisking round*)

Hey?

FATHER

Nothing, Captain.

[*Meanwhile the* MERCHANT *and the* GREEK GENTLEMAN *have wandered off left to look for the* JEWISH GENTLEMAN

LANDLORD

I'm sorry, my good man, I tell you it's absolutely impossible.

JOSEPH

I implore you, good host, in the name of all the Prophets . . .

LANDLORD

Be reasonable, man. I don't mean it unkindly. It can't be done, that's all. We're packed right out—aren't we, wife?

LANDLADY

Packed out? I should think we were. I'm sure I don't know how we shall manage as it is. Not an inch of space down here, as you can see for yourselves, and they're sleeping on the roof head to tail like herrings in a basket. Indecent, I call it. The Government's got no right to land poor innkeepers in such a pickle.

CENTURION

Now then, ma'am. What's the trouble here?

JOSEPH

Good soldier, can you help us to find a lodging for the night? We have sought everywhere in the town, and this is our last hope.

LANDLORD

And I'm telling him, Captain, we haven't so much as a corner. They'll have to push on to Jerusalem.

LANDLADY

It's only five miles, and it's a big place.

JOSEPH

Alas! sir, it's very late and a bad road. Will you not persuade this worthy couple to give us a shake-down somewhere? We are not particular. As you see, we are humble folk, and there are only the two of us.

LANDLADY

Yes, and like to be three of you before long, I reckon.

JOSEPH

Indeed, that's true. My wife is in no fit state to travel farther. Besides, our journey ends here.

LANDLORD

Captain, you can see we are not to blame——

CENTURION

Wait a bit, wait a bit. Let's get this straight. You, good master, what's your name?

JOSEPH

I am called Joseph ben Heli, and this is Mary, my wife,

CENTURION

Trade?

JOSEPH

Carpenter.

CENTURION

Place of residence?

JOSEPH

Nazareth in Galilee.

CENTURION

Lineage?

JOSEPH

Of the house and lineage of David.

CENTURION

Of David, eh? And this is the city of David?

JOSEPH

Yes, Captain.

CENTURION

And therefore the proper place for you to get yourselves registered?

JOSEPH

Yes, Captain.

CENTURION

I see. Well, it does seem a bit hard to move you on, especially as your good lady is so near her time. What do you say, landlord? Can't you shift some of the baggage and give them shelter under the arches?

[*During the following conversation,* MANSERVANT *and* MAIDSERVANT *bring in three braziers, placing one for the* MOTHER, *who uses it to cook supper, one just below the* HUSBAND *and* WIFE, *and the third near the* PHARISEE.

LANDLORD

Don't see how we can, sir. We've got all the servants of these ladies and gentlemen bedded down there as it is. You couldn't put a pin between 'em. It's not my fault if people will travel with such a lot of attendants. Inconsiderate, I call it, but there you are.

CENTURION

How about the stables? Is there any room there?

HE THAT SHOULD COME

LANDLORD

Well, I dunno about that. Let me see now—it means getting their ass in as well. Could you lie along of the ass, mistress?

MARY

Yes, indeed we could. She's a quiet good creature and gives no trouble, does she, Joseph?

JOSEPH

None whatever. Thank you kindly. A stable would be far better than nothing.

LANDLORD

I haven't promised anything yet. Let me put on my thinking cap. We can't move the camels, nor yet put the young gentleman's stallion in with the mares. Perhaps we could—— No! that won't work.

LANDLADY

Could we make room for the captain's gelding along of the merchant's she-asses—if you didn't mind, sir—

CENTURION

Not in the least. By all means.

LANDLORD

That's a good idea. Then we could put these people and their donkey in with old Ibrahim's draught-ox. How would that suit you?

JOSEPH

Excellently. We are greatly obliged to you.

MARY

It is most kind of you. We are sorry to be putting you to all this extra trouble on our account.

LANDLORD

That's all right. Don't like to think of you with nowhere to lay your heads. Especially under the circumstances, eh, wife?

LANDLADY

It's not that anybody *wants* to seem disobliging——

CENTURION

Of course not, of course not. Well, that's all settled. I'm sure you'll manage capitally. Good-night to you. (*He joins the* SOLDIERS *and confers with them.*)

MARY and JOSEPH

Good-night, Captain.

[*Here the* MERCHANT *reappears, left (L.U.), followed by the* GREEK GENTLEMAN. *They move along the passageway at the back.*

LANDLORD

Now you come along with me. I'll have some clean straw put down for you. (*Calling off right.*) Take the ass round to the stable! (*Hoofs heard off right and round to centre back.*) Mind how you go; you'll have to pick your way a bit. (*They move up back and across among the piled-up baggage in the passage-way.*) It's just across here and under the——

[*The* MERCHANT *falls over a pack-saddle, into the* LANDLORD'S *arms.*

Ouf! you might look where you're going, sir!

MERCHANT (*panting*)

I'm extremely sorry, Landlord. Could you tell me . . . Oh, dear! (*He is out of breath.*)

GREEK GENTLEMAN

Landlord, we are looking for a young gentleman in a green cloak. Have you by any chance seen such a one?

[JEWISH GENTLEMAN *emerges from stable, R.B.*

LANDLORD

This'll be him, sir, just coming through the archway.

MERCHANT

Oh, thank you, thank you!

LANDLORD

Don't mention it. (*He enters the centre stable with* MARY *and* JOSEPH.)

[LANDLADY *has meanwhile worked away left.*

MERCHANT

Sir! Pray, one moment, young gentleman!

JEWISH GENTLEMAN

Hullo!

GREEK GENTLEMAN

Your pardon, sir. This good merchant wishes to ask you—(*with a change of tone*) Now, by all the gods of Olympus! If it isn't my old friend Yussuf!

JEWISH GENTLEMAN

Philip! by all the Prophets! What on earth are you doing here? (*They come down right.*)

GREEK GENTLEMAN

Just travelling about. Studying social history and all that. Writing a little verse, and tinkering about with a magnum opus that will never get finished.

JEWISH GENTLEMAN

The same old Philip. Not changed a bit since college days. I'm delighted to see you. Come and sit down and let's have a yarn.

MERCHANT (*panting after them*)

Forgive me, sir, but I——

GREEK GENTLEMAN

Oh, yes, I forgot. This honest merchant wants to

know if he may have the protection of your company as far as Lydda.

[*Meanwhile* LANDLORD *may be seen taking straw in to stable, C.B.;* MAIDSERVANT *may take in water, etc., and fasten curtain of sacking across entrance.*

JEWISH GENTLEMAN

Certainly, by all means. The more the merrier. I hope, sir, you'll join us in a cup of wine.

MERCHANT

I am very much obliged, sir.

JEWISH GENTLEMAN

Here's a good place to sit in, near this worthy Pharisee. (*They all sit by* PHARISEE.) I trust we do not disturb you, sir. Thank you. Shockingly crowded this place is to-night, and I entirely agree with you, merchant, that travelling's no joke these days.

MERCHANT

Terrible, sir, terrible! Times are hard enough, goodness knows, without Caesar taking it into his head to number the people. Apart from everything else, look at the interruption to business. It's a sin and a shame——

PHARISEE (*interrupting*)

It is a sin indeed to number the people. It is the sin of King David, to which Satan provoked him. Is it not written in the Book of the Chronicles of the Kings of Israel?

GREEK GENTLEMAN

I have not studied the work in question, but I'll take your word for it.

JEWISH GENTLEMAN

You may take his word for it, Philip. He is a learned Pharisee, and he ought to know.

PHARISEE

Judging by your dress, gentlemen, and by the speech of one of you, you are Romans.

JEWISH GENTLEMAN

My friend is Greek, but I am as good a Jew as yourself, sir. I was educated in Rome, certainly, and prefer to dress in the fashion.

PHARISEE

God deliver us from the fashions of Rome—where they teach our Hebrew youth to sneer at God's word and bind a foreign yoke and a pagan custom upon our necks in flat defiance of the Law of Moses.

[*Throughout this conversation, the* LANDLORD, LAND-LADY, *and* SERVANTS *move unobtrusively about, looking after the travellers, who eat their supper and prepare for the night. Some of this action can be supposed to take place off, left, in attendance on people upstairs; and the* MANSERVANT *can go in and out of the stables. The* CENTURION *goes centre and stands behind the brazier warming his hands.*

Jewish Gentleman

Nonsense, sir! Surely one can be a sincere Jew and still live like a gentleman?

Pharisee (*contemptuously*)

Like a gentleman!

Jewish Gentleman

Yes, sir. I come of a good house, my father is a magistrate. I shall probably end up as a member of the Sanhedrim myself when the time comes. And when I'm there, be sure I shall press for a more enlightened and cosmopolitan policy.

Pharisee

Indeed, sir! Well, I am Zadok the Pharisee, a follower of Judas the Gaulonite, and I say that your godless Romanising policy is bringing upon this nation the curse due to the backslider and the apostate.

Jewish Gentleman

Upon my soul, sir——!

[*This little passage of arms attracts the attention of the* Centurion. *Seeing that it quiets down, he takes no action, but he keeps his eye on it.*

Merchant

Pray, gentlemen, don't quarrel. I'm a man of peace. I quite see your point, good Master Zadok. You're bound to look at things from the religious side. But I'm a plain man, and what I object to is the inconvenience. Here I am, torn from my home, put in peril of my life, and goodness knows what's happening to my business all this time! That scoundrelly Greek— Oh, I beg your pardon, noble sir—that manager of mine is probably making hay of the accounts, and I shall lose all my best customers. I'm a spice-merchant, gentlemen, Aaron ben Isaac is my name, in a pretty big way down at Joppa.

Pharisee

I'm glad you stick to the old-fashioned native name.

Merchant

Did I say Joppa? I meant Caesarea, of course. Caesarea we call it now, since Herod rebuilt it and made all those modern improvements. A heathen name, of course, but what's in a name?—and I must say, the King has succeeded in putting the town on the map. Here's my card, by the way, if you should happen to be requiring pepper, or perfumes, or anything in that line. I have the honour to supply nutmegs to the Imperial Household.

[*The* Landlord, *with a jug of wine in his hand, is now centre of stage. He serves* Husband *and prepares to go off left.*

Jewish Gentleman

Thanks very much. I'd be glad to know of any one who can supply bath-unguents and toilet-waters reasonably. The prices in Jerusalem are positively outrageous. Landlord! bring us some wine here!

[LANDLORD *returns with a jar of wine.*

PHARISEE

Bath-unguents, indeed! That's all you young men think about. It was a black day for Jewry when King Herod built the public baths for the corruption of our young men.

[*The* CENTURION, *smelling trouble, wanders casually up to the back of the group, with the detached air of a London policeman patrolling a public meeting.*

You loll about there all day, oiling your bodies and anointing your hair, reading lascivious heathen poetry, talking blasphemy, and idling away the time with Greek slaves and dancing-girls. May the curse of Korah, Dathan, and Abiram light on King Herod and his baths too. May the earth open and swallow them up.

LANDLORD

Your wine, gentlemen. (*Whispering.*) Sir, I implore you not to talk so loudly. King Herod's spies are everywhere. And the centurion is standing just behind you.

JEWISH GENTLEMAN

Serve to the gentlemen. Your health, sirs. Personally, I'm all for King Herod. He may be a bit of an autocrat, but he's done a lot for the country. How about his big housing schemes in Samaria, and Caesarea with its great new harbour and up-to-date drainage system?

MERCHANT

That's a fact. You wouldn't know the old place.

GREEK GENTLEMAN

I must make a point of visiting it.

JEWISH GENTLEMAN

Look at the Jordan Valley Waterworks. Look at the Temple in Jerusalem. Look at the theatres and amphitheatres the King has built and endowed——

PHARISEE

Nothing would induce me to look at them. Play-acting and wild-beast shows are an abomination in the sight of the Lord. Immoral, irreligious, and thoroughly un-Jewish.

JEWISH GENTLEMAN

Yes, they *are* un-Jewish. Our national attitude to the Arts is deplorable. King Herod is the only Jew in the country who cares twopence about cosmopolitan culture.

PHARISEE

Thank God for it. Nothing is so demoralising as art and culture. As for Herod, he is no true Israelite. He is an Edomite, a son of Ishmael, and, what's more, an unbeliever. He breaks the Law of Moses by letting the barbarians in the provinces put up graven images to him. And you, Aaron ben Isaac, who complain of the Imperial taxes, have you forgotten that it is unlawful to pay tribute to Caesar?

[*The* CENTURION *at this point really does take notice.*]

LANDLORD

Hush, hush, sir, for Heaven's sake!

MERCHANT (*alarmed*)

Here, I say! Hadn't you better be careful?

PHARISEE

You have no spirit. You are slaves, sold by Herod into the bondage of Rome—and all you can do is to sit there grumbling feebly about taxation and interruptions to business. What room will there be for such as you in the great day of redemption when the Lord's Messiah comes?

CENTURION

And what will your Messiah do when he does come?

LANDLORD

God of Abraham! I knew there'd be trouble. I'm sure, Captain, the gentleman means no harm. Don't hold it against me. This is a respectable house.

MERCHANT

Of course, of course, Captain. And anyway, I wasn't saying anything. I swear I haven't uttered a syllable against the Emperor or King Herod either. I never suggested the taxes were illegal. I only said they came heavy on a man, and so they do—but there's nothing treasonable in that.

Jewish Gentleman

That's what taxes are for—to give us something to grumble about. Eh, Captain? Sit down, man, and have a drink.

Greek Gentleman

That's right, Captain. Fill for the Captain, landlord.

Centurion

Thank you kindly, sir. I don't mind if I do. Cheer up, landlord, we're not going to crucify you yet awhile.

Landlord (*pouring wine for* Centurion)

No, sir. Thank you, sir. (*He retires, left.*)

[*Sound of singing and marching off, back.*

Centurion

Your health, sir! The gods be favourable to you. Cheer up, Master Merchant. So long as the taxes are paid, Rome can put up with a grumble or two.

Merchant (*with a wry face*)

Yes, yes, of course——

Centurion

And, after all, we do give you something to show for the money.

Pharisee (*sarcastically*)

Undoubtedly. Baths and theatres and drainage systems, and other worldly luxuries that our fathers did very well without.

Centurion

Better than that, sir. Peace and security. Listen!

Song of the Legionaries (*as they pass the inn*)

Bread and cheese, bread and cheese
Marching through Spain, boys,
With a sackful of loot
And a hole in your boot
At the end of the long campaign, boys;
Bread and cheese, bread and cheese

[*The* Roman Soldiers *join in for a bar or two.*

Early and late, boys,
For we'll get no cheer
Of beef and beer
Till we see the Julian gate, boys.
Beef and beer, beef and beer, etc. etc.

[*The song dies away off right, past the gate.*

Centurion

Those are the lads of the sixth, going up to keep order in Jerusalem. Good luck to 'em. And to King Herod too, say I. Regular good army man, is King Herod.

[*The* Merchant *endorses these sentiments with eager nods.*

Judaea was in a pretty mess till he took it over. He and the Emperor together have kept order these thirty years. No invasions, no civil wars, peace and prosperity and a reasonable check kept on bandits and insurgents. What more do you want?

PHARISEE (*with dignity*)

Peace is not everything. Prosperity is not everything. (*The* MERCHANT *tugs anxiously at his sleeve, but he continues*.) We want liberty for our nation and liberty for our religion.

CENTURION

Bless my heart, what do you think liberty means? Liberty to cut one another's throats—as you were doing before Rome stepped in and put a stop to it? There's no liberty in civil disorder. Liberty means freedom to go safely about your business and behave yourselves like good citizens. And you'll only get that under a strong central government. Do you think your Christ or Messiah or whatever you call him is going to beat Rome at that game?

PHARISEE

When the Messiah comes——

JEWISH GENTLEMAN

Need we argue about the Messiah?

MERCHANT

No, no, of course not. Let's keep clear of politics.

Greek Gentleman

Yes, but what is the Messiah?

Pharisee

When the Messiah comes, he will restore the kingdom to Israel and smite the heathen with a rod of iron.

[Merchant *groans*.

Centurion

I can't understand you Jews. Can't you live and let live? Nobody minds your worshipping what you please and how you please. The Emperor's very keen on religious toleration. We've got temples in Rome to all sorts of odd foreign deities, you'd be surprised; and if you liked to put one up there to your Jehovah, or whatever you call him, there's no reason why he and our Jove shouldn't get on capitally together.

Pharisee

The Lord God of Heaven is One God and One alone. We can make no compromise with idols.

Centurion

It seems to me you want all the religious liberty for yourselves and none for other people. Well, it's no affair of mine. But if your Messiah is proposing to start a war of religion——

Merchant

Really, now, really. *Do* let's leave the Messiah out of it. So far as I know, he isn't even born yet.

Centurion

Very sensible of him. If he takes my advice he'll put off being born for quite a little bit. King Herod has done a very tidy job keeping order in this province and he has no use at all for Messiahs and insurrections. Good evening. (*He marches off left, and is seen to speak to the* LANDLORD, *who follows him off.*)

[LEGIONARIES *heard again, singing :* " Beef and beer."

Merchant

Heaven preserve us! my heart was in my mouth. All this treasonable talk——

Jewish Gentleman

Zadok, do you never think that this stiff-necked resistance may end by destroying our nation?

Pharisee

Your easy toleration will end by destroying our souls. How long, O Lord, how long? (*He stalks stiffly away, and settles down left.*)

Song of the Legionaries

[*As the* LANDLADY *passes on some errand, the* 1ST SOLDIER *puts his arm round her. She pushes him off. Laughter.*

>Beef and beer, beef and beer
>Sitting at home, sweet home, boys,
>With a wench in your arm
>To keep you warm
>O take me back to Rome, boys!

MERCHANT

Men like that are a public danger.

[*Knocking off right, and sounds of argument with the* PORTER.

Oh, dear me! Are the soldiers coming in? Bear witness, gentlemen, I never saw him before.

[LANDLADY *extricates herself from the* SOLDIERS *and hurries off, right.* MERCHANT *retires to remote corner down left, below* PHARISEE.

SONG (*continued*)

Beef and beer, beef and beer,
And cram your bellies tight, boys,
For it's starve and freeze
On bread and cheese
When the eagles take their flight, boys.
Bread and cheese, bread and cheese, etc.

LANDLADY (*shrilly; backing in right*)

Now then, now then, what do you want at this time of night? It's no good, I tell you, my man. We're full up. Can't take anybody else. You needn't start arguing. We're full up.

1ST SHEPHERD

Excuse me, ma'am. My mate and me only looked in to see if we could buy a drop o' beer.

LANDLADY

Beer? Good gracious me, what next? This is an inn

for travellers, not a jug-and-bottle department. You must go to the wine-shop in the next street.

[SHEPHERDS *edge in after her.*

1ST SHEPHERD

The wine-shop's shut, ma'am, and we thought if you'd be so good as to oblige us——

LANDLADY

Nonsense. You must knock the wine-merchant up—or go without, much better for you. Get along now and don't hang about the doorway. You smell of the sheepfolds. Be off with you!

JEWISH GENTLEMAN (*calling upstage*)

Oh, for Heaven's sake, woman, stop screaming!

LANDLADY

Oh, dear! That's the young gentleman from Rome. Now he'll be vexed. (*Coming down.*) I'm sure I'm very sorry, sir; it's these common shepherds, pushing in here, wanting to buy beer, as if this was a vulgar alehouse. I've told them as plain as I could——

JEWISH GENTLEMAN

I heard you. Your voice, sweet hostess, goes through my head like a knife through a melon. Can't you give these honest lads their beer and have done with it?

[SHEPHERDS *advance hopefully.*

LANDLADY

We don't sell beer.

JEWISH GENTLEMAN

You grasp the idea, lads, don't you? We don't sell beer. What are you? Shepherds?

1ST SHEPHERD

Yes, sir. We weren't wishful to be troublesome. Me and my two sons be keepin' our sheep on the hills yonder, and, it bein' a cold sort o' night, Sam and me come along to get a little drop to our supper.

JEWISH GENTLEMAN

I see. Well, I haven't got any beer, but here's wine, if that'll suit you. Sit down and have a quick one before you go.

1ST AND 2ND SHEPHERDS

Thank you, sir. Very good of you, sir.

[*They gather about the* JEWISH GENTLEMAN—*he gives them wine.*

JEWISH GENTLEMAN

All right, hostess, that will do. (*Exit* LANDLADY, *working off left* (*L.U.*).) Now, tell me, my good friends, how are things going with you? Do you rub along pretty well? Or do you want a rebellion against the Government, and a new Messiah and all that kind of thing? You can talk quite freely to us. We shan't give you away. My friend here is studying social conditions, aren't you, Phil?

Greek Gentleman

Yes; I am very much interested in your Jewish religion and politics; but they are terribly complicated. This, for instance, your Messiah as you call him—what does that word mean, Yussuf?

Jewish Gentleman

Christos in Greek, Christ, the Anointed One.

[*During this long conversation, the rest of the travellers settle down to sleep. The* 1st Soldier *stands sentinel at the door, right; the other goes to sleep. The lights in the other two braziers die down, leaving only the group of the two* Gentlemen *and the* Shepherds *clearly lit, and a beam of moonlight on the stable door. Dim down front spots and No. 3 batten gradually.*

Greek Gentleman

Ah, yes. Messiah, Christ, I understand. Now, this anointed one—What is he? A king or a priest? Or is he some kind of hero or demi-god, after the fashion of our Hercules?

Jewish Gentleman

My dear man, these shepherds have never heard of Hercules.

Greek Gentleman

Never mind. I like to get the reactions of the common people to all these academic questions. What do you think of Christ, my good friends?

1st Shepherd

Well, sir, I don't rightly know. Some say he's to be a great prince, born of the royal house of David—him that was a king in Israel, you know, sir, long ago, wonderful rich and powerful, notwithstanding he began life as a poor shepherd, no better than us. But others say he'll be a mighty chieftain, more after the style of Judas the Maccabean, and lead a great rebellion against Rome. But I do hope and trust it won't be that way, sir—not in our time, anyway.

Jewish Gentleman

You don't want a rebellion, then?

1st Shepherd

That I do not, sir. Rebellions and civil wars and such never do no good to us poor folk.

2nd Shepherd

Come now, Father, I don't know. They say the Messiah will restore the kingdom and do away with oppression and taxes, and bring back the good old days, with milk and honey for everybody.

[*About this point,* Joseph *comes out of stable door (C.B.). He quietly wakes the* Maidservant, *who goes off left (L.U.), to look for* Landlady. Joseph *returns to stable.*]

1st Shepherd

Why, so he may; but there'll be a sight of poor souls ruined and slaughtered first. No; life's hard enough on the poor, as it is, without no wars. We're well enough off as we are, with King Herod. You'll find, sir, it's mostly the upper classes as complains about King Herod's government. He don't bear too hard on the farmers, all things considered. Of course some of the tax-gatherers puts the screw on cruel, but, saving your presence, gentlemen, I think they mostly gets their orders from the Emperor, and him living 'way off in Rome, maybe he don't quite know the way they go on here.

2ND SHEPHERD

Maybe, when Messiah comes, he'll explain matters to the Emperor. You know, sirs, there's some say he won't be a king at all—but a poor, good man, the servant of the people. Something more in the nature of a prophet, like, same as Elias, or it might be Nathan, what spoke and rebuked King David when he behaved so unjust to Uriah the Hittite.

[*Enter* LANDLADY, *left* (*L.U.*), *with lantern. She goes briskly in at stable door* (*C.B.*).]

1ST SHEPHERD

Yes, or a holy priest, more after the fashion of Aaron or Melchisedek, as will take away sin and bring the people back to righteousness—for there's a sad deal of worldly living these days, and men don't keep the Law as they did. Some of the young people don't seem to believe in nothing but dancing and going to prize-fights and having a good time.

2ND SHEPHERD

That's right. And there's a young chap I know,

that's employed in the theatre, as they call it, at Jerusalem, says the goings-on there is something shocking—men dressed up like women with masks on, acting heathen pieces full of smut and nastiness, and tumblers and chariot-races, and a terrible deal of betting and gambling. It ain't right, to our way of thinking. I expect Messiah will put a stop to all that.

[*The* CENTURION *reappears, left, and passes silently across the back of the stage, the moonlight catching his helmet as he goes past the stable. He goes out right.*

1ST SHEPHERD

Ay, so he will, I dare say. But he won't do it by making wars. People don't act holier in war-time, they acts more sinful. And what with soldiers stravaguing up and down, looting and pillaging and destroying the cattle and the crops, it's a bad business for everyone. No, we don't want no more wars.

GREEK GENTLEMAN

Upon my word, Yussuf, your countrymen seem to be very sensible fellows. Here's to you, shepherds, and I hope, when your Messiah comes, he'll turn out to be a prince of peace. If you ask my opinion——

[LANDLADY *comes briskly out of stable door, with* JOSEPH *following.*

LANDLADY

There now, didn't I tell you so?

JEWISH GENTLEMAN

Hullo! what's the matter with our good hostess now?

LANDLADY

It's no good talking that way to me, Joseph ben Heli; this is an inn, not a lying-in hospital. Of all the tiresome things! No, indeed I can't help you—I've got far too much to do. Perhaps there's some one among the company that can oblige. Excuse me, ladies, is there anybody here that's a midwife?

FATHER

Eh, what? Yes, my missus is a very good hand in that line. Wake up, Hepzibah, you're wanted.

[MOTHER *gets up*.

MOTHER

What is it? (FATHER *whispers*.) Oh, yes, of course.

LANDLADY

Very good of you, I'm sure. I wouldn't have had this happen for the world. It all comes of being softhearted and letting people in against one's better judgment. She's in the stable over there, in the far corner—you'll know it by the brown ox being there. Here, take this lantern.

JOSEPH

I'll carry the lantern to light the kind midwife.

LANDLADY

Indeed, my good man, you'll do no such thing. We don't want any husbands hanging around. This is a woman's job. Oh, dear! oh, dear! we shall none of us get any sleep to-night. And I don't suppose for one moment you thought to bring any proper swaddling-clothes with you.

JOSEPH

Yes, ma'am, indeed we came provided. The midwife will find everything needful in our saddle-bags.

[MOTHER *disappears into stable. The family group settles down again.*

LANDLADY

Well, that's a mercy. Bless me, what an upset!

JEWISH GENTLEMAN

Sweet mistress, do I gather we're expecting an addition to the company?

LANDLADY

Yes, indeed, sir, and I'm sure I'm very sorry for all this disturbance. It's this man's wife been taken with her pains, sir, and I really don't wonder, riding up all the way from Nazareth, and over these bad roads. It's a wicked thing, sir, isn't it, that decent folk should be jostled about and sent travelling willy-nilly, just because the Government takes it into its head to have a census.

1ST SHEPHERD

Ah! it's a shame, that it is.

JEWISH GENTLEMAN

Very trying indeed.

LANDLADY

We had to bed them down in the stable—along with the ox and the ass—and where we're to put the child, I really don't know. There isn't a cradle in the place. I had one, but I gave it to my daughter when she married. You'll have to use the manger, that's all. I'll go and find you some old sacking to line it with.

JOSEPH

God will reward you for all your kindness.

LANDLADY

Oh, well, it's all in the day's work, I suppose.

[*Exit* LANDLADY, *left* (*L.U.*).

1ST SHEPHERD

We'd better be getting along to the sheep now. Thank you kindly for the wine, sir. Good luck to you, Master Carpenter. May your good lady have a light childbirth.

2ND SHEPHERD

Ay, truly, and bring you a bonny baby to bless you.

JOSEPH

I thank you both from my heart.

[*Exeunt* SHEPHERDS, *right. Gate is noisily barred after them.*

Jewish Gentleman

Take courage, good man. These things happen every day. It's sure to be all right. Here, I'll have a wager with you. What odds will you lay me it's a boy?

Joseph

It would be robbing you, young sir. I know it will be a boy.

Greek Gentleman

Hark at him! Every father is certain it will be a boy.

Jewish Gentleman

And every Jewish mother is certain it will be the Messiah. Isn't that so, carpenter?

Joseph

That is so.

Jewish Gentleman

And what are you going to call your Messiah when you get him?

Joseph

His name shall be called Jesus; for he was so named of an angel before he was conceived in the womb.

Greek Gentleman

Jesus? and what does that mean?

Jewish Gentleman

Oh, it's quite a common Jewish name. It means liberator, a deliverer, a saviour—that sort of thing.

Joseph

He is to be called Jesus, because he shall save his people from their sins. The angel said so to his mother.

Greek Gentleman

He seems to have been a very communicative and explicit angel. What else did he say to your wife?

Joseph

He said, " The Holy Ghost shall come upon thee and the power of the most High shall overshadow thee; therefore that holy thing that shall be born of thee shall be called the Son of God."

Greek Gentleman

The son of a god. The expression seems very familiar. Our Greek mythology is full of such tales. Personally, I am an agnostic, but I am always willing to learn. Pray tell me, carpenter, did the god manifest himself in a shower of gold, as Jupiter did to Danae?

Jewish Gentleman

Be quiet, Philip. The God of Israel is nothing like your heathen deities. He is a spirit, and works, not after the flesh but after the spirit. Besides, your own philosophers will tell you that your Olympic myths are themselves no more than symbols of the working of the spirit upon the flesh.

Greek Gentleman

So they say, indeed. But I believe the whole thing is nothing but a pack of fairy-tales.

Jewish Gentleman

I don't know, Philip. Sometimes I have wondered whether the Son of God, when He comes, might not fulfil your prophecies as well as ours. The hearts of all men have felt obscurely that God should somehow reveal Himself—walk as a man with men—I do not know. Does not Euripides speak somewhere of a Zeus that should know human suffering?

Greek Gentleman

Yes; in the *Eumenides*. But I thought your God was rather an exclusive deity, and never troubled Himself about any but His chosen people.

Jewish Gentleman

I know. But we insist very loudly that He is God of the whole earth. One would expect Him to take some interest in the outlying portions of His dominions. What do you say, carpenter?

[PHARISEE *gets up and comes across right.*

Joseph

I do not know at all, sir. I am a plain ignorant man. I try only to do my duty and obey the word of God without asking too many questions. But here is a

Pharisee coming across to us. He is no doubt learned in the Scriptures. Perhaps he can tell us.

Jewish Gentleman

Why, if it isn't my old friend Zadok. You seem to be restless, sir. I hope our talk hasn't disturbed you.

Pharisee (*with more concession to common humanity than he has shown up till now*)

The snoring of Aaron ben Isaac the merchant is a curse more intolerable than all the ten plagues of Egypt. The bellowing of fat bulls of Bashan is silence by comparison.

Greek Gentleman

You have come in time to settle a theological argument. My friend here says that the God of Israel is lord of the whole earth, and in consequence the Messiah will be the saviour of the Gentiles as well as of the Jews. Do you support that opinion?

Pharisee

Certainly not. It is blasphemous and ridiculous. He will set his foot upon the necks of the nations, and the heathen will be cast into outer darkness with wailing and gnashing of teeth. I hope you are answered. This inn seems to be very noisy to-night. I am going outside to try and get a little peace and quietness. (*He goes out by door to stair, left (L.U.), passing* LANDLADY, *who goes into stable (C.B.).*)

Greek Gentleman

What a very dogmatic person! It must be marvellous to feel so positive about everything. I never feel certain of anything.

Jewish Gentleman

That is the malady of you Greeks—you are blown about with every wind. Ours is to shut ourselves up tight in tradition and exclude every breath of fresh air. If only we could somehow wed the purity of our religion to the intellectual vigour of your philosophy! Well, never mind. Sing to us, Philip, and take our minds off our worries.

Greek Gentleman

Will it not disturb the company?

Jewish Gentleman

If they can sleep through each other's snoring, they can sleep through anything. Sing softly.

Greek Gentleman

Very well. (*Sings*): "Golden Apollo—" (*He breaks off; to* Joseph, *politely*): You will excuse my singing about Apollo. The words are of no importance, but the tune is pretty. (*Sings*):

> Golden Apollo,
>   lord of the burning bow,
> Thy brow with sacred fillets bound
> And deathless laurel crowned;
> Singer and seer, whose splendour lights the sun,
> Sweet, terrible one!
> Swift as the swallow
>   thy searching arrows go.
> Then smite, lord, smite the heart of desire
> With thy celestial fire.

[*The* Centurion *comes in, right, and speaks to the* Sentry, *who wakes his companion to go on guard in his place. The* CENTURION *picks his way slowly across the stage, lending momentary attention to the song and going to stand by entrance left.*

 Master of vision
   throned on the circling wheel,
 Immortal born of mortal birth
 That once didst visit earth
 And as a servant humbly walk with men;
 Turn, turn thee again,
 Mighty physician
   Whose hand can harm and heal,
 And quench, lord, quench thy heavenly dart
 For it doth rive the heart.

[MERCHANT *rolls over with a loud snore and snort; they all laugh.*

JEWISH GENTLEMAN

There is the comment of the commercial mind. You may rive his ears, but never his heart. Try again.

GREEK GENTLEMAN

There is no more to that song. Take the lute yourself.

JEWISH GENTLEMAN

I will sing you an old Jewish tale. (*Sings. After verse* 1, *the other two join in the chorus*) :

 Adam and Eve stood under a tree,
   (*Four rivers in Paradise*)
 A sweet and comely sight to see
 For they were fair as fair could be,
 Adam and Eve beneath the tree
   (*Paradise, Paradise,*
   God is all in all).

And on the tree the branches grew
    (*Four rivers in Paradise*)
Adorned with leaves of tender hue,
And they were fair as fair could be
And Adam and Eve stood under the tree
    (*Paradise, Paradise,*
    God is all in all).

[*An ox lows.*

Joseph

Listen! What was that?

Greek Gentleman

Only an ox lowing. Sing the next verse.

Jewish Gentleman (*sings*)

And on the branch a beauteous flower
    (*Four rivers in Paradise*)
Budded and bloomed from hour to hour,
The flower that on the branches grew
Adorned with leaves of tender hue,
And it was fair as fair could be
And Adam and Eve stood under the tree
    (*Paradise, Paradise,*
    God is all in all).

[Centurion *goes out, left.*

And in that flower a fruit of gold
    (*Four rivers in Paradise*)
Lay hid within the petals' fold,
The petals of the beauteous flower
That budded and bloomed from hour to hour,

The flower that on the branches grew
Adorned with leaves of tender hue,
And it was fair as fair could be
And Adam and Eve stood under the tree
    (Paradise, Paradise,
    God is all in all).

[*An ass brays.*

Joseph

Listen again.

Greek Gentleman

It is only the braying of an ass. Go on. Never mind the competition.

Jewish Gentleman (*sings*)

But Eve put forth her hand anon,
    (Four rivers in Paradise)
And bit that fruit unto the stone,
The strange, forbidden fruit of gold
That hid within the petals' fold,
The petals of the beauteous flower
That budded and bloomed from hour to hour,
The flower that on the branches grew
Adorned with leaves of tender hue,
And the tree withered down to the ground so bare,
And Adam and Eve stood naked there;
    (Paradise, Paradise,
    God is all in all)

But when the stone had fallen to earth,
    (Four rivers in Paradise)
It brought another tree to birth,
That tall and stately grew anon,

The tree that sprang from that fruit stone,
The strange forbidden fruit of gold
That hid within the petals' fold,
The petals of the beauteous flower
That budded and bloomed from hour to hour,
The flower that on the branches grew
Adorned with leaves of tender hue,
And it was fair as fair could be,
And Adam and Eve stood under the tree
>   (*Paradise, Paradise,*
>   *God is all in all*).

Greek Gentleman

Well sung, all! There is nothing like music to pass the time away. How goes the night?

[Centurion *reappears, left (L.U.)*.

Joseph

It is the dark hour before the dawn. Hark!

[*The cry of the Child is heard.*

Jewish Gentleman

That sounds more like it. Congratulations, carpenter.

[*Enter* Landlady *from stable.*

Greek Gentleman

Here comes our good hostess, grinning from ear to ear. How about it, mistress? What's the news?

Landlady

Come hither, Master Carpenter, and see! Your good lady is lighter of a splendid son.

JOSEPH

Praise be to God!

JEWISH GENTLEMAN

I should have lost my bet. Congratulations again. So you were lending a hand after all, hostess? You seem very much pleased about it all.

[CENTURION *works his way down on left.*

LANDLADY

Well, sir, when it comes to babies, even innkeepers has their feelings. And the dear mother is such a sweet person—it's a pleasure to do anything for her. A beautiful child, and both doing fine. Come along, father, and have a look. You'll be that proud you won't know yourself.

JOSEPH

The dayspring from on high hath visited us.

[JOSEPH *follows the* LANDLADY *into the stable. The* CENTURION *crosses briskly left to right in front of the platform.*

JEWISH GENTLEMAN

Well, well—that bit of excitement's over. Hullo, Centurion, you still on the prowl? Have you heard the glad tidings? The carpenter's wife has presented him with a son.

CENTURION

The gods be favourable to the boy!

GREEK GENTLEMAN

And there you are! Kingdoms rise and fall, wars are

waged, politicians wrangle, trade suffers, poor men starve, philosophers exchange insults and agree in nothing except that times are very evil and mankind rapidly going to the dogs. And yet, when one more soul is born into this highly unsatisfactory world, everybody conspires to be delighted.

Jewish Gentleman

And every time his parents are persuaded that he's going to turn out something wonderful, whereas, if they only knew it, he's destined, as likely as not, to finish up between two thieves on Crucifixion Hill. It all makes me feel very old and disillusioned.

Centurion

Dont' you worry, sir. You'll get younger as you get older.

Greek Gentleman

At any rate, I suppose we can now hope for a little sleep.

[*Knocking at the gate.*

Oh, Hades!

Voice (*without*)

Now then, what the devil do you want?

Voices (*without*)

Let us in! Let us in! We have news, news, news!

Centurion

News? What does that mean? (*Shouting.*) Porter! open the gates! (*Softly.*) Might be a rebellion. You never know. Look alive there! (*He moves up behind the two* Gentlemen. *The* 1st Soldier *springs to his feet*

HE THAT SHOULD COME

and joins the 2nd SOLDIER *at the entrance. The* LANDLADY *enters from the stable, and the* LANDLORD *from the left.*)

LANDLORD

A rebellion? God forbid! (*Shouting.*) Keep the gate shut!

LANDLADY

Oh, please, dear Captain, don't let them in! We shall all be murdered in our beds.

CENTURION

If there is news, we must hear it. (*Shouting.*) Open the gate.

[*Gate unbarred.* SHEPHERDS *enter noisily;* the SOLDIERS *bar their way.*

Now, then, fellows! What's all this noise about? (*He signs to the* SOLDIERS *to let them through. They stand guard again behind the* SHEPHERDS.)

SHEPHERDS

Show us the Child that is born to-night! For we have seen a miracle.

MERCHANT (*waking suddenly*)

Hey! hey! Robbers! murder! help! Keep off! Let me go! I'm only a poor traveller! I've no money on me! Help! help!

[*Everybody wakes up. Tumult.*
[*Bring* SHEPHERDS *centre and bring up arena flood slowly to full during their story.*

Centurion
Be quiet, there!

Jewish Gentleman
It's all right, Aaron ben Isaac. Nobody's being robbed.

Landlord
You've had nightmare.

Greek Gentleman
It's only some shepherds, who say they're seen a miracle.

Merchant
Miracle, indeed! I thought I was being murdered. This inn is disgracefully run. I shall complain to the authorities.

1st Shepherd
Indeed, indeed, sirs, a wonderful thing is come to pass.

Merchant
Oh, go to Gehenna! (*He rolls himself up again and resolutely closes his ears.*)

Centurion
Quick, fellows! Your story.

1st Shepherd
Sir, we were in the fields, keeping watch over our sheep this night. And as I sat, looking eastward toward Beth-Shemesh, I beheld a great light, as though the sun were rising an hour before its time. And even while I looked, my son Matthew spoke to me, and said:

Father, said he, what is this? Is the sun rising in the west? Then I turned myself about, and saw as it might be a ring of fire, all about the earth, and the hills and trees glowing like copper in the furnace.

2ND SHEPHERD

Ay, and the fire burnt up and up to the very pole, putting out the stars.

3RD SHEPHERD

And out of the fire, out of the sky—I cannot tell how, but so it was—there came an angel, great and terrible and shining. And we were sore afraid.

2ND SHEPHERD

Ay, that we were. But the sheep weren't afraid, not they. And that's a strange thing too.

1ST SHEPHERD

Then the angel spoke, clear as anything. " Be not afraid," he says, " for behold I bring you glad tidings of great joy which shall be to you and all people. For to you," he says, " is born this day in the City of David " —that's here, sir, you know—" a saviour, which is the Lord Messiah."

JEWISH GENTLEMAN

You hear, Philip? The Lord Christ. Zadok the Pharisee should be listening to this. What's become of him, by the way?

GREEK GENTLEMAN

Oh, he cast himself into outer darkness some time ago.

Jewish Gentleman

"Joy to all people"—you are sure the angel said, "to *all* people"?

1st Shepherd

Certain sure, sir. And we was just thinking as how there might be a many babes born in the city, and how was we to know, when he says, "This", he says, "shall be a sign to you. Ye shall find the babe wrapped in swaddling clothes and lying in a manger." So I looks at Sam, and Sam looks at me, and then, all of a sudden we sees the heavens open and thousands, ah! millions of angels, more than a man could count and singing that beautiful—Oh, sirs, listen! listen! There it be again—going right away over the roof, as clear as clear.

Angels' Choir (*distant*)

Glory to God in the highest and in earth peace, good-will towards men.

[*Repeat chorus, crescendo and dying away again; dim arena flood to about ¼ as song passes.*

Pause.

Centurion

Look here, I don't understand a word of all this.

1st Shepherd

Couldn't you hear nothing?

Centurion

Not a word.

Greek Gentleman

Nothing whatever.

LANDLADY

They've had too much to drink, that's what it is. You didn't ought to have given them that wine, sir.

JEWISH GENTLEMAN

I don't know. I fancy I did hear something—but it was very faint.

CENTURION

This is all a pack of nonsense. Go home, you shepherds, and let's hear no more of this. (*He turns to the* TRAVELLERS, *who are beginning to talk.*) Quiet, everybody. Get back to bed. Show's over.

[*The* TRAVELLERS *subside.*

1ST SHEPHERD

But may we not see the Child?

CENTURION (*after a brief hesitation*)

You may see him. But for his own sake, don't let your story come to King Herod's ears.

JEWISH GENTLEMAN

Come with me, shepherds. I'll show you the way. (*He leads the* SHEPHERDS *up centre.*) Listen! That is the Mother singing to her son.

[*The* CENTURION *sits on edge of platform, a menacing black shadow between the audience and the brazier.*

The curtain before the stable-door is withdrawn to disclose the HOLY FAMILY. (*Take out spot batten.*)

The GREEK GENTLEMAN (*lost in the shadows*) *has picked up the lute and accompanies* MARY'S *song.*

MARY (*sings*)

Balow-la-lee, my little king,
  What shall we do to comfort Thee?
Canst Thou for whom the angels sing
  Content Thee with balow-la-lee,
              Balow-la-lee?
Balow-la-lee, my royal child,
  There's little we can give to Thee,
A manger-bed, a mother mild,
  The ox and the ass for company,
              Balow-la-lee.

[1ST *and* 3RD SHEPHERDS *on the side of stable-door ;* 2ND SHEPHERD *and* JEWISH GENTLEMAN *on the other.*

1ST SHEPHERD

Your pardon, mistress. May we come in and see the Baby?

MARY

Surely, good shepherds. Come in and welcome.

JOSEPH

Tread softly. Do not wake Him.

MARY

He is already awake. Look, He is smiling at you.

1ST SHEPHERD

All hail, little king! See, here is a woollen fleece to be your royal robe.

2ND SHEPHERD

All hail, little king! Here is a shepherd's crook, to be your royal sceptre.

3RD SHEPHERD

All hail, little king! Here is a twist of flowering thorn to be your royal crown.

MARY

My Son shall remember you all when He comes into His kingdom.

JEWISH GENTLEMAN

Madam, I fear I have come unprovided. I was not expecting a revelation. But if ever your Son and I should meet again, I will have a rich gift ready for him.

MARY

Sir, we shall not forget your goodwill. What is your name?

JEWISH GENTLEMAN

I am Joseph of Arimathaea.

[*The* SHEPHERDS *play a pastoral tune upon their pipes, and the Tableaux* CURTAINS *close. From behind:* Landlord! landlord! . . . Up, you lazy slaves! will you lie there till noonday? . . . Saddle the asses and bring my reckoning. . . . Oh, dear, I never got a wink of sleep all night. . . . Has anybody seen my slippers? . . . Confound you, sir, you've knocked my flask over. . . . Git over, hoss—ah! would you then? . . . You have overcharged me by five pence. . . . Landlord! landlord! (*fading away*).

[*If gauzes are used, drop them on* NATIVITY TABLEAU, *blackout and let voices fade off in the dark; then bring up spot on forestage as* KINGS *re-enter.*

BALTHAZAR

Caspar!

CASPAR

Melchior!

MELCHIOR

Balthazar!

CASPAR

I looked for wisdom—and behold! the wisdom of the innocent.

MELCHIOR

I looked for power—and behold! the power of the helpless.

BALTHAZAR

I looked for the manhood in God—and behold! A God made man.

CASPAR

Up and to horse! Make haste! for the Star has moved on before us
And the east is pale with the dawn. We must ride by faith.

MELCHIOR

Following the light invisible.

BALTHAZAR

Following the Star.

CURTAIN

(or, if there is no front curtain, the Kings go out left).

THE DOROTHY L. SAYERS SOCIETY

THE DOROTHY L. SAYERS Society, with now some 500 members worldwide, was founded in her hometown of Witham in 1976. Its aims are educational: to collect and preserve archival material, to act as a centre of advice for scholars and researchers, and to present the name of Dorothy L. Sayers to the public by encouraging publication and performance of her works and by making grants and awards. We have close links with the Marion E. Wade Center at Wheaton College, Illinois, where the majority of her papers are held.

An annual Convention is held with at least half a dozen further meetings not only in UK, but we have also met in USA, Germany, Sweden, France and The Netherlands, studying themes ranging from Incunabula, fungal poisons and Dante, to Education and the Nicene Creed. We have held concerts of music, have sponsored performances of The Zeal of thy House in Canterbury Cathedral, the Bach B Minor Mass in Oxford, and new incidental music for our production of some of The Man Born to be King plays in London. 1993 saw the Centenary of the birth of Dorothy L. Sayers with over 30 events worldwide. Her poem "The Three Kings" was set as a carol, and performed and broadcast in the Midnight service at Canterbury Cathedral.

Our publications include the Poetry of Dorothy L. Sayers, five volumes of The Letters of Dorothy L. Sayers, and, most recently, two hitherto unpublished talks by DLS, Les origines du roman policier, and The Christ of the Creeds. We have extensive archives.

Witham now has a Dorothy L. Sayers Centre in the public library where we hold an annual Sayers Lecture and a statue of DLS with her cat Blitz.

Further information is available from the Society's headquarters at Rose Cottage, Malthouse Lane, Hurstpierpoint, West Sussex BN6 9JY or the web site: http://www.sayers.org.uk

Christopher Dean
DLS Society Chairman
2011

www.ingramcontent.com/pod-product-compliance
Lightning Source LLC
Chambersburg PA
CBHW070514090426
42735CB00012B/2771